A Wife Fighting Against All Odds – A True Story

By
Mable Collins

Copyright © 2023

All Rights Reserved

Hardcover ISBN: 978-1-164953-984-7

Paperback ISBN: 978-1-64953-918-2

Dedication

This book is dedicated to my spouse, Darrell Collins, for without him, I could not have made it through every hardship. Our love story would not be complete without me. Additionally, I dedicate it to all the women and men who are facing challenges, fighting against all odds, and making all efforts to help their spouses get back on their feet.

Acknowledgement

I would want to express my thanks to my closest friend Diane White Harden for constantly telling me that I can succeed and for supporting me on this path.

Patricia Alpha was a great team player who was willing to lend me her spot to shine that day when I wanted to do an interview in her home. I would want to thank her for that.

We succeeded, despite her comment that "my voice doesn't sound right."

My spouse doesn't doubt the assistance of my niece-in-law Claudia Hilton and her uncle Steven Hilton; they were there for her when her uncle didn't have a wheelchair. I would want to thank them both.

Thank you to Susan Licausi for becoming a member of my team. She was really helpful in setting up the camera, and I took footage while sitting in her seat.

I would want to express my gratitude to Marva Hilton for always being supportive and wanting me to succeed in my endeavors.

I am grateful to Laura Sibley for always being there for me when I needed someone to talk to. She never turned me away and listened to me. She also told me to keep writing, girl, and I *appreciate your support in helping me succeed in writing these books.*

I must express my appreciation to Shaniera Hassan. You made this possible for me; you worked so hard to edit my book and were extremely patient with me even when I wanted to yell at you. I am so grateful for the way you conduct business with clients like me. Thank you once more.

Thanks Dad for believing in me, the challenge I faces and was able to overcome it. Will missed you 12/8/2024.

About the Author

Life is a journey, full of ups and downs, and along the way, we find companions who walk with and beside us. My highs were surrounded by a sea of faces, and with the lows, the crowd thins, but I just need to remember it's during those challenging times that the truest colors shine through. It is a reminder that while some may fade away when the clouds are grey, some stay steadfast, offering a hand to lift you. It is a stark reflection of my life as it unfolds, where the support of others often surges during the bright days but wanes when the storm clouds gather. My narrative is centered around my husband's stroke; it speaks to the profound impact of such an experience. As a mother of three children, I always wanted to write, but I was so busy with them since I wanted them to get a good education. At the age of 60, I discovered that what I really wanted to do with the rest of my life was to write and provide details of my experiences after my husband suffered a stroke, which put me in a position to want to fight for the disabled people who were unable to help themselves through these difficult times. My story is everyone else's story, but I reacted with a positive state of mind. I stand up for my beliefs and encourage others to do the same. Never give up even if you feel like you can't accomplish something or are having a hard time because help is out there if you just take a leap of faith and keep trying until you succeed. I will never give up the struggle for the stroke victim since they need us in their life.

TABLE OF CONTENT

Dedication..ii

Acknowledgement..iii

About the Author...vii

Chapter 1..1

Life is Not Meant to be Easy; It is Meant to be Lived...1

Chapter 2 11
The Months of Stresses and Hardships *11*

Chapter 3 37
Life is a Test – Darrell's Sickness Made Me Stronger *37*

Chapter 4 60
Fighting all Odds to Comfort Love of My Life *60*

Chapter 5 86
Trying Everything to Offer Darrell Best Possible Treatment *86*

Chapter 6 94
The Death of My Beloved Son *94*

Chapter 7 106
New Year – New Hopes *106*

Chapter 8 123
Taking Some Time Out to Shed Off Stresses *123*

Chapter 9 140
Darrell's Medical Condition Severed *140*

Chapter 10 151
Therapeutic Treatment for Darrell – Diagnosis of Osteoporosis *151*

Chapter 11 170

Life Challenges Continued *170*

Chapter 12 179

Life Gave Some Reasons to Smile *179*

Chapter 13 189

Life Is Still Testing Darrell and Me *189*

Chapter 14 208

Happy Days Were Just Knocking *208*

Chapter 15 224

Hard Time Finding a Reliable Therapy Service *224*

Chapter 16 240

Watching Your Love Smiling is Best Ever Feeling ... *240*

Chapter 17 246

There were Still Some Challenges *246*

Chapter 18 261

Some Relaxing Time *261*

Chapter 19 267

Although Unpleasant but Some Relations Persists ... *267*

Chapter 20 280

Christmas and New Year – Life is Gaining Back Colors

....*280*

Chapter 21 285

***Narrowly Escaping a Scam** 285*

Chapter 1

Life is Not Meant to be Easy; It is Meant to be Lived.

"You only live once but if you do it right, that is enough."
~ **Mae West**

In February 2014, my husband visited a doctor to find out what was wrong with his kidney. After his primary physician informed him that a cyst had been discovered on his kidney and was beginning to grow, the specialist wanted to perform additional tests, and we went back and forth to the X-ray room because it was difficult to see clearly on the film, which put my husband in a panic.

I was quite concerned about his health, but I had to acknowledge that the situation was beyond my ability to influence him in any manner.

It can be difficult to convince another person not to stress about their condition, especially if that person is your husband. To confirm that it was not cancer, the primary care physician instructed him to get it checked once every six months while it continued to grow. It started little but picked up speed as the weeks and months passed, and at that time, my husband was struggling with anxiety over the prospect of death. I told him that I believed God intended you to stay here for long.

Then, after about six months,

after a detailed checkup, the physician informed him that he had two cysts on both kidneys. He also recommended some additional tests. These tests confirmed that he had cancer in both kidneys. My husband ran out of his house in frustration after knowing about his disease.

I know one thing: my husband believed in God, so when he was back, I sat with him, and we discussed about the situation. I told him if you are scared that the enemy may step in like a knife, pray to God because He has his best interests in mind, and He will always be on your side. I advised him, "Keep living your life and not allow it to disintegrate. I will be there for you every step during the way. No matter what happens to you, whether good or bad, I will always be there for you and will look after you when needed." So, at that point, we could only wait to find out what would happen next.

September 2014

<u>*Brother-in-law's Unfortunate Death*</u>

In **September 2014**, my husband's younger brother suffered a heart attack. His girlfriend attempted to transport him to the hospital, but he passed away just as she was about to bring him in. He was pronounced dead at the spot by the paramedics.

On **29 September 2014,** my husband left the house immediately to provide assistance to his brother girlfriend. In the meantime, his other brother also arrived to lend a hand. I stayed behind because I was responsible for watching our grandson while our daughter went to work. It was a difficult day because my brother in law had left behind a young daughter. However, the family rallied together to assist in any manner that they could be of use.

My husband decided to stay in California until the situation became normal since he is a kind of person always willing to lend a hand to others, regardless of what others comment about him.

After a couple of weeks, I got ready to go to the funeral. I went there with my daughters, grandson, and son. We all paid our respects to Michael, my brother-in-law. He was a really annoying, both in what he said and in what he did.

Michael had a pleasant demeanor. He could make you laugh, and he could also make you angry. I will never forget that sometime before his death, we all went to Las Vegas with his brother and his girlfriend. Throughout the trip, we laughed and spoke nonsense so much that I wanted them to be quiet for some time. But from the time I recall spending with my spouse, they have consistently done that. My internal feeling went something like this: "Blood is thicker than water, but not in like their mess, brothers."

Just to give you a little background on how those two got along as brothers, I will let you get back to what I was saying about how we all went to the funeral to meet my husband. The funeral went off without a hitch. There was no turmoil, and everyone went their separate ways after saying their goodbyes.

Chapter 2

The Months of Stresses and Hardships

"Stress acts as an accelerator: it will push you either forward or backward, but you choose which direction."
                        ~ Chelsea Erieau

April 2015

Sudden Illness of Our Son

In **April 2015**, another tragedy occurred

when my son became ill; however, I was

unaware of it even though I continued to receive repeated phone calls to inform me about my son getting sick. But unfortunately, I could not attend those calls. His heart was at 8 percent, and he needed to be airlifted to the hospital in Stanford from Monterey, California. When a roommate got in touch with me, she gave me the phone number, and when I called it, I was informed that my husband and I needed to reach the hospital immediately. It frightened me and my husband, and as we walked into the hospital, both of us were crying and holding each other. Our son was overjoyed that we would visit him very soon. My niece, nephew, and great-nephew travelled to visit him. My husband's nephew and niece-in-law also followed us immediately. During that difficult time, he had the support of his family. My husband and I stayed there until he recovered fully. After his operation, our cousin Barbara and his great-aunt Viola, arrived. After a little while, my sister Carolyn E. arrived to visit our son with a friend Lynden, she is my son auntie Carolyn E whom visited him. Having to adapt took a lot of effort and time during that month. After he fully recovered, we decided to reside in the flat with our son. It had been about a month, and my husband was all set to leave shortly. Then, he received a phone call about the critical condition of his elder brother in

Colorado spring, and he spoke to his brother as he was leaving this world. Although it was tragic, my husband, his niece, and his brother had travelled to Colorado spring before his brother passed away. They went out to eat, and while there, they ensured he was taking care of his business before he left. Since he was in the army at the time, he did not have too many things to worry about, and I was able to talk to him during those times. He had a great sense of humor, especially when people asked him questions. He would ask them if they were the police or something else. It was very funny at times, but there were a lot of incidents. At that time, I decided to stay with my son in Monterey, California, until **15 August, 2015**, and will leave afterwards. While my husband had already gone and boarded the plane. I visited Darrell Jr. in **June 2015** and helped him with his residence. I cleaned up his apartment and assisted him in changing his sheets so that he could have a pleasant stay. After having him rest and wash his clothes, we got up the following day. My son told me: "You snore and he can't bear it, so you sleep in the bed and I will stay on the couch." I responded with "no," then he said, "I do not want you to wake up the roommate because she has to go to work in the morning." Then I replied, "Okay, but are you sure? I want you to be comfortable in your bed," he said, "Yes". Therefore, he went to sleep on the couch while complaining to my son, "Your mother is unable to control her snoring." We accomplished a lot together as mother and son. For example, I administered an injection of the blood thinner heparin he needed to prevent blood clots, and my son wore a holster monitoring device. I indeed shopped for him. He was unable to transport any hefty bags at all. I am thankful I was there with him when his roommate had an ugly fight one morning. A big woman entered the home while I had the door open so that someone could clean the carpet for us. The woman appeared out of nowhere and hit the man in the room where my son's roommate and his boyfriend were present. I told my son to go to his room because I did not have time to deal with the situation, but his roommate ran behind me to my son's room while her boyfriend was being beaten. I was afraid because by then, after everything had been said and done, the roommate was talking mess, but the big lady was gone and it was over. I commented that this shouldn't have happened when I was at my son's apartment because he was unaware of what was going on and had just returned home from hospital. I felt extremely uneasy being in that house. To maintain my sanity through this trying time for my son and myself, I found it necessary to read my bible every day. Every morning, I would serve him breakfast, prepare a meal for dinner, and check to see that he had a balanced and nutritious meal every time. Additionally, every two weeks, we were required to travel to Stanford Hospital to check on how well his heart was functioning. The absence of blood clots was a positive indicator, and there was no infection despite an open wound while I was tending him, which was fantastic. The brother-in-law of Darrell's brother, Steve was willing to lend us one of his automobiles so that we could take my son to the Stanford hospital when it became necessary, which turned out to be very helpful. Then, my son expressed interest in going back to work as quickly as possible to start paying his debts. I told him he needed to wait a bit because he was on sick leave, but he said he used to be busy working all the time, hence, I went with him to Starbucks. The following week, he returned to work with his doctor's permission. I couldn't leave his place since it was so peaceful, so I began cooking Darrell's meals for the week there. I wanted to encourage him to maintain a balanced diet by teaching him how to cook nutritious food. So, I believe this time. I had two and a half weeks. I went to pick up Diane in Pittsburgh, California, to come and stay with us for three days. He is crazy for Diane so I had to bring her over there to see him. I prepared dinner for all of us, and we all enjoyed it very much. It consisted of bean bake, chicken rice, salad, and water. The next morning, we all travelled to the Monterey fishermen's dock. After searching most of the store, I purchased some Ghirardelli chocolate candies. We all went to store to buy many items there. After that we went for a long walk. My son Darrell enjoyed that very much and was a good exercise for all of us too. While doing so, we sat, talked, and laughed. We also went to view the seal on a small beach that Monterey has. It was an indeed lovely sight to watch. The weather was windy as usual, most expected in Monterey, California. I always love walking with the people whom I love and enjoy spending my good time with. We had a great time together when we were out on the town, so after I dropped Diane off the following day, Darrell came along for the ride as we travelled back to

Pittsburg, California, to drop her off at her home. After I dropped her at her home, Darrell Junior and I went inside to greet everyone else, and then we got back into the car to begin the long drive back to Monterey, California. It was quite late, and it seemed like we had a long way to go, but I just kept i driving. When we finally reached there, I was exhausted and took a shower to relax. After that, I went straight to bed. On Sunday, I attended church with my son and his friend, where we heard an enjoyable sermon. As soon as we got home from church, we sat down to a meal that I had prepared for all of us. After that, we took some time to relax, so we would be able to get up early so that I could take him to the doctor since he had a day off from work on Monday. Although I do not like driving in traffic, it was crucial that he must go to the doctor so that I can determine how long I will be staying in California with my son and ensure that he is capable of recovering and looking after himself. The morning, we got up to some fantastic news: the doctor told me to stay here until **15 August, 2015.**

My next plan was to go to the beach with my son and his friends. One of his friends birthday was approaching on the same date as my niece. We went to Santa Cruz beach in California for the birthday. We cooked, sat together, and talked a lot. I was the only old lady there but my son wanted me with him since I had to do his shots heparin for blood clots at a certain time. It brought him so much joy to have me there to tell them that his mother had arrived to join them at the beach. However, I also had a good time because I was able to observe how these college students and young adults connect while socializing without any evidence of drinking. When you hit the ball over the net, they played ball while we sat on the beach. When it was time to depart, boys, it was difficult for me to walk through all that sand, but I managed to get out of there. We took a pleasant ride back with Nickki, who dropped us off at her place so that we could pick up my son's car. I followed Darrell all the way back to his house. He went back to work the next day. He was 8 hours per day and 40 hours per week. On Friday, 8 August 2015, we had to travel to Sanford Hospital again for Darrell's junior check-up. It was essential to see how well he was recovering then, So we reached out to the hospital at our scheduled time. At night, my niece, Demeka, contacted my son Darrell and invited us to her birthday. He wanted to go to the Birthday party in Oakland at a club. I agreed to his wish. It was a nice party, and we enjoyed ourselves there. I saw that my brother Pee-wee was looking really sharp. I was extremely impressed to see him dressed up; it had been some time since I had last seen him, and everyone had a good time. My son, Darrell, enjoys spending time with his extended family and friends, and he said he did have a good time hanging out with my older brother. Several days later, I boarded the next flight to Arizona, to return to my home, feeling exhausted but relieved that my son was recovered and safe now. When I got back, my dad angrily waited for me since he needed me to get for certain tasks. He was whining as usual, even though I had just gotten back. I commented, "Give me a break; I had just gotten back". But the following day, I assisted him with whatever he required and took him to the FRYS grocery to get his prescription. Finally, I got to hang out with my spouse, including playing poker with him, which is something he really enjoys doing. While hanging out with the guys and gal that played poker every night, occasionally, he works for

Jason, who is the one who runs the games. Darrell will help him with setting up the table. He had not yet gotten over his anxiety about the operation that would be performed on his right kidney in September. He made a brief statement on the matter just before it was time to go in for it. On **9 September, 2015,** my husband underwent surgery at Banner Hospital to have cancer removed from his kidney. On the same day, I received a call from a friend informing me that her Great nephew had passed away, and my heart burst into a million pieces. After that, my husband was yelling around the hallways, and the nurses wanted him to be quiet since he was talking out of his head under that anesthesia. I was upset because I had just learned that my husband was acting strangely because of the drug. After giving him a goodnight kiss, I drove home and told him I would see him the next day but needed some rest first. Therefore, I returned home to lie down and get some rest. I returned to the hospital in the afternoon to check on him, and he appeared to be doing well at that point. I told him I went back home to prepare for him and my dad at the house. Then I placed the food up after my dad had taken his meal because the doctor said that if he seemed to be doing good, he would be discharged from the hospital. So, I said, "I will pick you up tomorrow". **On 12 September 2015,**

Darrell was released from the hospital, and we had to retrieve his prescriptions from the pharmacy at Banner Hospital before continuing to our residence.

Chapter 3

Life is a Test – Darrell's Sickness Made Me Stronger

"Life is a test, make sure you study for it."
~ R.J. Intindola

January 2018

<u>**My Husband's Chronic Illness**</u>

In the frosty month of **January,**

Darrell found himself faced with a daunting journey. It was **2018,** and within his body, a battle was raging. Once a vital organ, the left kidney had fallen prey to the hidden clutches of cancer. Determined to reclaim his health and restore balance to his being, Darrell made the courageous decision to undergo surgery. With hope in his heart and a team of skilled medical professionals by his side, he embarked on a path towards healing. The surgery had been a success, and his recovery was progressing smoothly. A month had passed since that fateful day in January, and now it was the **27 February, 2018**. Darrell, a young man with dreams and aspirations, found himself caught in the midst of a terrible car accident. The impact was so forceful that it caused him to be violently thrown from the van, leaving him in a state of shock and disbelief. My husband was visibly speechless and behaving strangely when a Buckeye Police officer brought him home.

On a frigid winter's day, on **28 February, 2018,** a strange sensation grasped my senses as I observed the demeanor of my dear husband, Darrell. It was apparent that something was wrong, casting a shadow of unease upon the atmosphere. His usually cheerful demeanor gave off the impression of having been quiet, giving way to a look that was disconnected and worried. I made the decision to act and look for assistance for my love out of concern for him. I did so with a heavy burden in my chest as I set off on a quest to find the help that Darrell required. It was not an easy task as negotiating the complex landscape of mental health services proved to be a difficult hurdle to overcome. But I kept going because I was determined to see Darrell become the person he once was. As the days grew into weeks, I diligently investigated the complexities of the healthcare system, making sure to investigate every possible avenue in my search for a solution. In my search for guidance, I turned to the wise counsel of professionals and sought comfort in the affection of support networks.

At the beginning of **March**, we had a visit from a nurse practitioner who came to our house. This appointment was planned in order to carry out a comprehensive assessment of Darrell's current health status. However, as the nurse practitioner continued to go deeper into the examination, Darrell began to get a growing sensation of discomfort. It seemed as though something wasn't quite right. The nurse practitioner suggested me get a medical and general power of attorney for my husband. At that time, Darrell's state of mind might still be described as being positive.

April 2018

Darell Suffered a Stroke

Until the early hours of the **21 April**, **2018,** around 2:30 in the morning, Darrell flatly refused to get any kind of medical treatment. The body of Darrell was found lying on its back, and he was unable to utter a single sound. Then, one of my children brought up the possibility that their father had a stroke while we talked about it. After calling for emergency medical services and waiting for them to come, it was decided that Darrell should be transported to Abrazo Hospital, where he stayed for approximately two weeks while receiving medical care. It was established that Darrell was suffering from a stroke after further testing was carried out.

I needed sometime to collect my thoughts and get cleaned up before going to the hospital to check on how my spouse was doing. When we initially encountered Darrell, he did not give off the impression that he was in very good condition at all. When I tried to chat with Darrell, he did not respond to my attempts to engage him in conversation; rather, he continued looking upward into the air the entire time I tried to talk to him. During my discussion with the attending physician, I found out that Darrell was given medication to help reduce the symptoms of the stroke and protect his brain from any extra damage that may have been induced as a result of the stroke.

Later on, after I got back home, around three in the morning, I got a call from Sunview Health Care informing me that Darrell had been transferred to their hospital and that I needed to come in and sign the proper documents. The call came shortly after I had returned from the hospital myself.

When I arrived at the Sun Health Rehabilitation center, my husband, Darrell Collins, was laying on the floor, and a nurse was standing above him, pumping a thick milky fluid into his stomach. When I left, the nurse was still there. It appeared to me that my partner was being dealt with an attitude similar to how people in a third-world country may be treated. It was unpleasant and disturbing for me to observe my partner in such a powerless situation as he was at that time.

After that, I informed members of Darrell's family about what was going on despite the fact that I did not have a crystal-clear picture of how things would turn out for Darrell. Soon after my husband suffered from stroke, one of his niece's, Clandria Hilton, drove all the way from Los Angeles California to Suncity Arizona, to see him. She had a great time with her uncle Darrell, played some music for him, and also FaceTime with her other Uncle Steve and Auntie Debbie so that they could also see him. Due to stroke my husband might not have recognized her but still he looked very happy upon seeing Clandria. Due to her visit, I also felt encouraged and relieved in those difficult times.

During this time, a member of the billing staff made several attempts to convince me to enroll Darrell in a hospice program; however, I turned down their offer because I did not believe it was appropriate for me to treat my husband in such a manner.

The lady repeatedly tried to persuade me that if Darrell accepted hospice care, he would be allowed to stay in the hospital and would receive additional medical attention. Because I made the decision not to enroll my husband in hospice care, my family and I have been harassed by the hospice through a series of phone calls and home visits. This was all because of my decision not to enroll my husband in hospice care. We were given the ultimatum that either we would have to take him checking out of the hospital or come up with a payment of $10,000 for services that had already been rendered. My husband had become mute and was unable to walk, so the only other option that was provided to us was to place him with a group of strangers in a setting that he was not familiar with. We had no idea what would happen to him there.

During the time that I was receiving hospice care, I made sure they were aware that the one and only thing I desired for my husband was for him to undergo rehabilitation to be able to return home. After two weeks, Darrell's progress in physical therapy and speech therapy had been encouraging, and to know that my husband was participating in these therapies brought a huge smile to my face. After having these services given for a period of one month, the services were discontinued since there was an insufficient amount of financing of $10,000.

The massive bill for services that

Darrell was having, could not have been paid because we did not have the essential financial resources. Since we were unable to pay Darrell's medical expenses, he was in danger of being discharged from the hospital. After the hospital contacted me regarding the payment for these treatments, they also started calling our daughter at her place of employment to inquire about the same matter. Because of this, the difficulty of the situation significantly increased.

This made me feel a little uneasy. After going through such a scary situation, during which it was unclear whether or not my husband would be able to acquire appropriate care owing to our lack of financial resources. In the long run he was receiving benefits before this, he never filed an application for social security; I decided to submit an application for Darrell's assistance from long term.

I informed Social Security that I had applied for long term help for Darrell; however, after I did so, I was never contacted by them again. Despite my disclosure, I never received aid from long-term care. The worker consoled me by relating that she had been through a similar experience with a member of her own family and assuring me that she would do everything possible to aid me with Darrell's condition. This happened when I started crying and explained the scenario to that particular staff woman. I then broke down in tears. After that, the social security caseworker who was assisting me informed me that a representative of long-term care would get in touch with me within the following week. The case manager for long-term care gave me a call on the next business day after she had received my message. I was informed that for Darrell to be able to give me with long term services, it would be necessary for me to move him into a local care facility as quickly as possible. Someone who works at the facility provided me with this information. When it was time to bring him out of the Sunview Rehabilitation Center in Sun City, I was so enthusiastic that I could barely contain it. Being under constant financial stress was a really terrible experience for me, and I lacked experience in this area because no one I was close to had ever suffered from a stroke before. It was just my blowing.

Chapter 4

Fighting all Odds to Comfort Love of My Life

"You're still the one that I love/The only one I dream of."
         ~ **Shania Twain**

June 2018

<u>**Shifting Darrell to Palm Valley Rehabilitation Center**</u>

On **11 June, 2018,** I signed the Release for Darrell to be moved from Sunview to Palm Valley Rehabilitation

Center. It is located in Avondale, Arizona and is just at a distance of about 15 minutes from my home. When I found out that my spouse had moved closer to us, I couldn't help but feel joyful and relieved at the same time. Darrell started off by taking part in both physical therapy and speech therapy at the beginning of his treatment. At first, the social worker there was really easy to talk to and offered very helpful advice. The only way he would be able to receive care at the Rehabilitation center was if he admitted to having dementia to be moved to the appropriate section of the facility.

I made it a point to check in with Darrell every single day to see how he was progressing and how things were going overall.

July 2018

<u>Ms. Hilton's Death</u>

Both Darrell's physical treatment and his speech therapy were showing signs of improvement in **July 2018**. He was regaining the ability to walk with the support of others, taking it one step at a time, and he was also starting to feed himself.

Because my spouse was unable to make it to the funeral of Ms. Hilton **in July 2018**, I was required to take a little trip away from home so that I could pay my respects. My spouse greatly admired her because she was such a well-respected woman. My closest friend went to the funeral with me to offer her condolence. . It surprised me when his younger brother-in-law welcomed me and Diane with a warm hug and expressed his happiness at seeing me again. During our time there, his brother-in-law was a big help in making us comfortable. After the burial, we went to her son's house to be with him and his family for the rest of the day. Her sons did an outstanding job of setting things up, and of course, one of his brother-in-law's spouses also pitched in to help out.

Therefore, when went to the Hilton family's house to complete the funeral and were on our way back to her residence, she said, "I will drive. We will get a rental automobile. I'll assist you in filling up the gas tank." My friend Diane decided that instead of letting me fly back to Arizona by myself, she would go with me. This was a better option for her. We had a few hours of travel ahead of us before making a brief visit at a casino because I wanted to ensure that everything was in order since I was planning to bring my husband back home after a couple of months i.e., in **October 2019.** While we were going back to Arizona on Highway 10, we sang some of our favorite songs. As we drove up the highway into Los Angeles, California, I overheard some rumors that had been going around. The name of the gambling place was the Spot 29 casino. My friend Diane went there, and as soon as she arrived, she began hitting every machine in the room singing to her. She triumphed as though there had been no one else present. She won $500.00 that evening by nine o'clock. We stayed there for a while before leaving.

It started to rain and thunder as I drove back to my house Buckeye, Arizona, where I had been. She insisted that I look up at the sky so that I could see the dark clouds that were above us, but I wouldn't. After driving for another two and a half hours, she made a small stop at the gas station. Then, I had to carry on with the rest of the drive to home. We felt frightened when the thunder started as soon as we arrived at my home in Buckeye. As a result, we hurried to park the car inside the garage because it was pouring heavily outside. Finally, we were successful and filmed everything. When Diane first started to hear noises, she looked out the window and thought she saw someone outside my home.

My response was simply, "Who" Diane mentioned that whenever you call me on the phone, you always say that you are hearing something outside your window. I stated that that is how I feel whenever I am alone. There was an air conditioner in every window. When she said that someone was in the room, the wind blew the cardboard off the wall, and she began running so fast that she almost knocked my butt onto the floor. As I entered the second room my chest began to tighten with anxiety because I had just observed that the cardboard was beginning to peel off. My friend Diane was yelling, so I told her to quiet down and wait until morning in my room. I was terrified, but I knew I had to be brave because I had to continue, so I thoroughly checked it to ensure it was not something terrible.

    After bearing that for too long, we

were successful in getting some sleep before fulfilling our duty to bring the rental car back to company in the next morning. After that, we made our way to the nursing home to see Darrell. In the later part of that month, we introduced him to his poker friends, and he couldn't contain his excitement when he saw them. Seeing that they made the trip to see him was very satisfying. The level of play was significantly improved, thanks to Jason's excellent work. It made me feel uneasy because the nurse had assured me that Darrell would be dressed nicely; however, when I looked at him, he was wearing a lady's blouse with jeans and a rubber medical glove to keep his pants up. The nurse was just provided with a mild warning the following day. My friend fell ill the next week, so she made sure to get plenty of healing and rest time. As a direct consequence of this, my father kept calling to inquire about speaking with

Diane, whom I regarded as both a sister to me and a daughter to my dad. After initially suspecting that I was making up her illness, he eventually realized it was genuine after driving over to check on her. After that, he engaged Diane in conversation and conveyed his desire to take her out to lunch or dinner if she started to feel better. As soon as Diane began to feel better, we resumed our normal activities, including going to the local casinos while adhering to a limited diet. She joined me for my workout at the gym, after which we both enjoyed our meal, which was roughly the size of the palm of your hand, which we shared. As soon as she arrived, she began spending a lot of time adventuring in parts of the city she had never visited before. I even went so far as to drive her to my dad's church on Sunday. While a female pastor was at home praying during a storm, she shared her thoughts on the thunder and lightning occurring outside. In addition to that, there was a great deal of singing. Diane and I laughed it off as though she was exaggerating the situation, despite the fact that it was nighttime and, as a result, a tornado was approaching. They looked at a person's face, which surprised me because I was aware that it was not funny. After she had finished her sermon, we put some money on the offering plate. After we left the building, my dad reached into his pocket for the money.

August 2018

Darrell's Physical Therapy

In **August 2018**, there was a verbal argument regarding Palm Valley's decision to stop Darrell's participation in physical therapy. Because of this, I decided to begin looking for an outside therapist for Darrell.

After beginning his treatment in **December 2018**, I was finally successful in convincing Darrell to start attending his physical therapy sessions outside of Swans in **January 2019.** Darrell attended the Swans for physical rehabilitation services beginning in **January 2019** and continuing through March 2019. During this time, I was granted permission to bring Darrell to my house for visits and meals. After being taken out for a daytime lunch and visit on **30 March, 2019,** around five o'clock in the evening, Darrell was brought back to Palms Valley Rehab Center to continue his treatment.

Shortly after delivering Darrell to the treatment center, he suffered an epileptic fit. When Darrell experienced the seizure while at the Palm Valley Rehabilitation Center, nobody promptly administered medical assistance or asked for assistance when needed. I found out about it when I received a phone call from Lisa, a person I met at the Palm Valley Rehabilitation Center. Lisa was the one who called the paramedics after the registered nurse failed to do so on her own initiative. I thank God that Lisa informed me that my husband was having a seizure. She also informed me that she had called the paramedic to take him to the emergency room at Abrazo Hospital, which is located directly across the street. The registered nurse simply stood there and observed him while he was lying on the ground. My daughter drove all the way to Palm Valley so that we could get a better understanding of what had transpired, including the fact that Darrell had a seizure and the nurse chose not to call the emergency services.

The nurse acted as if she shocked because she had never dealt with a seizure before and was unsure of what to do in this particular situation. I got up and left without continuing my conversation with the registered nurse in any way. After I left, I was confused and depressed because I had taken my husband out for Chinese food and a fun night, only to return home and learn that he had a seizure while we were out. I got depressed when I asked the emergency room where my husband was and they told me that he was in the intensive care unit (ICU). I hurried over with my daughter and her boyfriend to find out what was happening with him at this point.

When we arrived, there was a limit of two people who could enter at once. When I found Darrell, he was lying on his back with a tube entering his stomach and a nearby breathing machine. As a result of the decreased blood flow throughout his body, the soles of his feet had taken on a charcoal-like appearance. Before she broke down into uncontrollable tears, my daughter yelled, "Dad, can you hear me?" Although she was crying her eyes out, I realized to keep my composure for the sake of my daughter. When I turned to look around, I saw that Darrell's clothes had been taken off and were lying on the ground. I questioned the physician about Darrell's prognosis and inquired about the possibility of restoring his circulation. They told me that although he would leave soon, he would stay there for some time. In addition, I was cautioned against taking Darrell back to the Palm Valley Rehabilitation Center at any time. It was instructed that I should make an effort to relocate him because customers come here for emergencies similar to this one, which can lead to death. Hence, I made an effort to move him.

I paid attention, and the following day, I enlisted the help of several of my close friends so that I could remove Darrell's clothing. Because I was concerned about Darrell getting a feeding tube or a peg implanted in his stomach, I looked for a new facility for him to go to for a while, and I went there every day to check on him. Meanwhile, he was still in the old facility. After I had a conversation with the caseworker, Andrew agreed to assist me in locating a new rehabilitation center where I could put Darrell until we were either in a position to bring him home or find a more suitable facility.

Chapter 5

Trying Everything to Offer Darrell Best Possible Treatment

"It's always better when we're together."
~ Jack Johnson

April 2019

<u>*Darrell's Admission to Estrella Care Center*</u>

On **15 April, 2019**, Darrell was admitted to Estrella Care Center, and I thought it was such a hopeful sign for his future. After I had dropped him off at his destination, my friend Susan and I got in the car and drove to see him. He had not fully recovered from the grand mal seizure yet, but he was making progress. After he had finished getting settled in at the Estrella Care Center, one of the registered nurses there took down all of his information. After that, she informed me of who would be his C.N.A. and then inquired as to whether or not Darrell smoked cigarettes. I explained to her that he had a seizure and wasn't in any condition to smoke; he was there for his illness. When I informed her that he must not smoke, she immediately left the room.

I think she was able to hear me. The next day, I went back to the Estrella Care Center to request Darrell to get speech and physical treatment. I had a conversation with the speech therapist. He came in, closed the door, and began saying that, to the best of his (the therapist's) knowledge, Darrell would never be able to eat or speak for himself again despite the fact that he had been doing both of those things up to that point. In fewer than two months, I started assisting Darrell with eating himself.

After that, the speech therapist was given permission to observe Darrell when he fed himself. He wanted Darrell to be able to advance to other types of therapy in his presence, such as physical therapy, so he kept Darrell in the rehabilitation center while he was there. The patient had to first go through a swallowing test before the physical therapist would even consider starting the patient on any kind of physical therapy. In addition to this, I asked the medical staff to remove the feeding tube from his body. The registered nurse told me that they would see him after the test, something that had never occurred to him before. As a direct consequence of this, the speech therapist at Banner Hospital carried out the evaluation with the assistance of a machine. If I had not brought him to the clinic, they never would have thought to run the test in the first place. Therefore, somewhere around the middle of June, my husband took all the tests. After that, somewhere around **24 June, 2019**, I left to attend a birthday party for a friend's ex-husband, who is no longer with us. There was a family gathering on or around **29 June,**

2019. It was a nice and engaging experience overall. Everyone joined the Soul Train line while we were dancing and chatting away at the same time. I could catch up with a few old friends I hadn't seen in a while. Being invited to participate in this event was a privilege.

July 2019

Taking Out Some Time for Myself - Visiting My Niece Home

When my sister Diane and I went to Hayward in **July 2019** to visit my niece at her house, I got to spend time with both my family and my friends. Everyone was encouraged to come and join us. The idea of hanging out with my son Darrell Jr. made me feel an overwhelming sense of contentment. I was unconscious that this moment would mark the last time I would see my son while he was still alive.

Chapter 6

The Death of My Beloved Son

"Come back. Even as a shadow, even as a dream."
~ **Euripides**

March 2020

My Son's Death

On **10 March, 2020**, I made my first appearance in the world, but I had to say goodbye to my son since he had a heart problem. My son worked at a coffee shop, and the owner of the shop reached out to me over Facebook with a message. She recommended me to get in touch with my son and inquire about what was troubling him. When I called my son's mobile phone, the person who answered was from the Monterey County authorities. The police officer who picked my call quickly questioned "Are you Darrell's mother?" To which I responded, "Yes, I am." He then told me that your son has passed away. I started crying and yelling wildly at the same time. I then contacted my children, nieces, and nephews about the death news of Darrell Jr., my son. At that time, my husband (participating in some form of physical therapy with the assistance of a caregiver. Unfortunately, I had to ask caregiver that, given the circumstances, it would be best if she went back to her own house.

When the caregiver refused to go, I informed her that I needed to have a very private conversation with my husband and that I did not want to have that conversation in front of her at that time. She continued to stand there. Because of the nature of the circumstance, it was necessary for just my family and I to be present there. After leaving the house hesitantly and with a great deal of displeasure on her face, the caregiver stormed out of the house.

Not long after that, I received a phone call from the caregiver's employer informing me that they would no longer be caring for my husband. As a direct consequence of this, I was required to take care of my spouse all by myself so that I could pay my final respects to my son and achieve closure. After some time had passed, Darrell Sr. and I had a conversation in which I broke the news to him that our only son had passed away, and that we would never see him again while he was still living. Even though I was used to having

Darrell Sr. by my side, I had the distinct impression that I was all by myself as I cried since my husband, who is non-verbal, was unable to convey the sense of loss that I was experiencing at the time. After getting in touch with my daughters, the grandkids and their paternal grandma showed up shortly thereafter. She said a few things during her visit that I found to be very hurtful and sad to me, given that I had just recently laid to rest my only son.

It has always been a mystery to me how another person could say something like, "Cry it out now that you understand how I felt when I lost my son." My annoyance, which was already quite high then, was aggravated by such comments. In the end, I was able to forgive her because I realized that when people pass away, others may occasionally talk without first carefully analyzing what they are going to say. This came to mind the trip that When

Darrell's relatives came to visit in **February 2020**

Ridiculous Comments of people

In this circumstance, I was forced to deal with other people's ridiculous comments once more. It was explained to my husband that if he didn't start walking and talking soon, no one would come back to see him. This comment was meant to be addressed to my spouse in particular. Who would commit such a terrible act? Throughout the rest of **2020** and the entire **2021**, the primary focus of my attention was on monitoring the progress of my husband's physical therapy. My left thumb was scheduled to undergo surgery on the last day of **2021**. Because of this, I was unfortunately compelled to place Darrell in a residential care facility, despite the fact that doing so was the last thing I wanted to do. To my regret, I did not have any other options. After a number of months of searching,

Darrell's case manager still did not find a suitable care provider. Before I left my husband at the assisted living facility, I prayed for his protection and hoped that he would be okay there.

December 2021

My Hand Surgery

On **17 December 2021**, I went in for surgery on my left hand because a bone that was growing from my thumb was causing me a great deal of discomfort and was pressing on a nerve. When my good friend Susan drove me home from the hospital following my operation, I was overcome with a sense of loneliness. Because of this, I was left without any practical means of taking care of myself or my spouse (if he had been at home at the time). Since I was unable to acquire any assistance from a home health aide with preparing food, cleaning, or even making my bed, I felt like I had no control over the situation at all. I needed help from a neighbor in order to eat in an appropriate manner, so

I went to ask for it. I was not even capable of chopping up ingredients to prepare meals.

Even better, a neighbor of mine offered to drive me to the nursing home so that I could visit Darrell.

Chapter 7

New Year – New Hopes

"Whatever has happened in the past year, the New Year brings fresh beginnings."
       ~ **Peggy Toney Horton**

January 2022

<u>A New Year with Great Hopes</u>

As the clock struck midnight on the eve of **1 January, 2022,** a wave of celebration and excitement swept across the globe. The air was filled with overwhelming anticipation as people bid farewell to the challenges and uncertainties. This year, I found myself spending most of my days in the peace of my home. It was a time of self-reflection and personal growth, as I got the opportunity to focus on myself and recover from my surgery. Despite my husband's non-verbal condition, I gathered the courage to ask a friend if they would accompany me on a visit to see him. The thought of driving myself filled me with fear, as I doubted my ability to maintain control of the steering wheel in case of an accident.

Consequently, I have spent most of this month keeping myself occupied at home and watching some television when there is something on that I may be interested in. After the holiday break, I started taking my grandchildren back to school. It wasn't that far, about 15 minutes away, and I drove very carefully. In this cold month of January, fate dealt me a cruel hand as I found myself caught in the chaos of an unforeseen accident. As I travelled along the bustling street, my attention was momentarily captured by the vibrant landscape that surrounded me. The traffic light ahead cast its direct shadow, compelling me to stop my vehicle. Little did I know that an unexpected encounter would soon disrupt this seemingly ordinary pause. Out of nowhere, a car reached behind me, its engine humming with anticipation. To my surprise, it was not the vehicle owner who occupied the driver's seat but rather his daughter. In a twist of fate, she carelessly collided with the back of my car, jolting me forward in my seat. The sudden impact sent shockwaves through my body, leaving me momentarily confused.

As I cautiously navigated my car to the side of the road, the concerned father emerged from the car, his face filled with concern. He approached my car, his eyes scanning for any visible signs of damage. Then, he noticed a wire sticking out from the rear, a clear sign of the collision's after-effect. With a comforting tone, he offered his assistance, assuring me that the damage was minimal and could be easily rectified without involving insurance companies. His confidence in his ability to repair my car was visible as if he naturally understood its inner functioning. At that moment, I found myself torn between the convenience of his proposal and the unrelenting voice of caution in the back of my mind. Should I trust this stranger's expertise and allow him to repair my vehicle, or should I adhere to the convenient path of contacting my insurance company? While considering my choices, the street was alive with the buzz of vehicles going by, completely ignorant to the problem being played out in front of them.

The decision lay solely in my hands, a choice that would undoubtedly shape the course of events that followed. I firmly expressed my refusal, stating that I needed to contact the insurance company. I was concerned that there might be additional issues with my car, beyond what he suggested. Reluctantly, we proceeded to exchange our driving licenses and addresses, ensuring that all essential information was shared.

After encountering the reckless driver, I made my way back home, eager to resolve the matter with the insurance company. I reached for the phone and dialled their number with a sense of urgency, hoping to provide them with the additional information they required. As I spoke to the representative on the other end, I carefully provided every detail of the incident, ensuring that no crucial information was left out. It was important for them to clearly understand the events that had transpired so they could assess the situation accurately. Once I provided all the necessary information, the insurance representative assured me they would promptly contact the responsible party's insurance company.

After that, someone from the insurance company came out to take pictures of the damage, and after that, the company located a repair shop for me to take it to, and they arranged for me to have a rental car for the next thirty days while it is being fixed. After that, I drove the rental car around, picking up kids and dropping them off at their respective activities. McKayla's gymnastics class meets three times a week, and she looks forward to coming there and having fun with her piercing. Consequently, we continued our monthly routine without changing it. At the end of the previous month, my daughter brought up the possibility of taking the children to Disneyland. It was a surprise as part of Messiah's birthday, and she asked me to keep the surprise to myself and not let him know about it in any way. I have continued bringing my grandchildren to school and then, their activities after school.

Messiah began participating in basketball practice in the middle of January since he enjoyed playing sports in general. The coach said that this guy was a natural and surely knew how to handle that ball and that Messiah was terrific defensively as well. So, he was hitting the ball in the basket, and he went there twice a week. Therefore, McKayla and I continued to sit there while watching her brother play. When he finished, we took the long trip back to the motorways and drove to my daughter's house to drop the kids off. After that, I headed back to my home to get some rest before trying to clean my house with one hand while wearing a cast, but I managed to get it done somehow. Finally, I used to shower and get ready for bed so that I could wake up early enough to drive them to school in the morning.

We were quickly approaching the **final day of January**. I was relieved that we were almost there, so I would have another cast applied when February arrived. The first one was a soft cast wrapped around my hand after surgery, and it itched so much that I wanted it off since it made my hand hot and uncomfortable. Because my nerve was being pinched by the broken bone in my thumb, which will now be fixed, I was relieved that the discomfort in my finger, caused by the nerves pressing down on other nerves, would no longer be an issue. My daughters asked if I could bring the recently purchased SUV truck to Los Angeles California for Disney land to which I happily replied "Yes".

When I asked my friend Susan if she might stop over and see how my husband was spending those days while I was out of town, she enthusiastically agreed to do so, and I proceeded to make the necessary arrangements. I began to pack little by little to prepare myself to travel to Anaheim, California when the time came, but I still had to keep quiet until my daughters got the big surprise of where they were going to in March before my husband arrived that month, so I kept quiet. This helped me decide to plan the trip with my daughters and grandchildren. I thought it a good chance to spend valuable time with my daughters and grandkids in my old age.

Chapter 8

Taking Some Time Out to Shed Off Stresses

"It isn't how much time you spend somewhere that makes it memorable: it's how you spend the time."
                         ~ David Brenner

March 2022

The Joyful Tour of Disneyland

In **March**, my daughter presented my beloved grandchildren with a delightful surprise: a trip to the captivating world of Disneyland. This unexpected gift was in honour of Messiah's upcoming birthday, which falls on the **8 May**. It was a thoughtful present, granting the children an early celebration to remember. The pure happiness radiated from their faces, evident by the bright smiles covering them. Their excitement was evident as I collected them in the early morning hours, preparing to take them to school. They both eagerly tried to convey their excitement simultaneously, their words falling out in a jumble of enthusiasm.

In the following weeks, we stepped into the beautiful state of California. With the break of dawn, we set out on our adventure, seeking comfort and new experiences. Our trustworthy companion, my truck, was carrying us through the winding roads. The snacks were neatly packed, ready for our adventure to begin. As I turned around, a wave of joy spread over me as I saw the sheer happiness on my grandchildren's faces. They clutched their white t-shirts tightly, eager to have them signed by the beloved characters of Disneyland. Our journey had brought us to California, and our first stop was the magnificent Santa Monica Beach. It was an important day for my grandkids, who had never experienced the wonders of a beach before. Born and raised in Arizona, the allure of the ocean was a thrilling prospect for them. The excitement in the air was noticeable as we approached the sandy shores of Santa Monica Beach in California.

The children walked along the sandy shore, their laughter filling the air as they soaked in the wonder of the beach. They delighted in the simple pleasure of building sandcastles, their tiny hands shaping the grains into amazing structures. Running towards the crashing waves, they cried out with delight, their youthful energy propelling them forward. Time seemed to slip away as they immersed themselves in the carefree joy of the moment. For an hour and a half, they ran around and played. As the sun shone brightly overhead, we spent some memorable time on beach.

We enjoyed a lot playing in the sand, creating castles, and digging trenches. The waves crashed against the shore, providing a soothing soundtrack to our relaxing day. As we strolled along the coastline, we saw a group of individuals engaged in an interesting activity. People were capturing interesting scenes with their cameras. Curiosity piqued, we paused momentarily, observing the view ahead of us. It was a fascinating view, but soon, we realized it was time to continue our journey. Our destination? The adventurous world of Disneyland in Anaheim, California. With excitement bubbling within us, we made our way towards the park. To our delight, my daughters discovered a convenient path that led directly from our hotel to the entrance of Disneyland. It was a stroke of luck, allowing us to embark on this magical adventure easily.

Upon reaching our accommodations, we took a moment to settle in. My grandkids were thrilled to have their own room. Perhaps we should have opted for a suite, but nonetheless, the cozy quarters provided a comfortable haven for our stay. The children's happiness radiated throughout the room. It was evident that this experience would forever be in their memories. And so, as the day drew to a close, we sat together, basking in the contentment that enveloped us. The anticipation of the days ahead filled our hearts, knowing that this journey would be filled with unforgettable moments and cherished memories. I was filled with joy as I reflected on my precious moments with them. After the whirlwind of excitement had subsided, we decided to satisfy our hunger with a delicious meal. As we took each bite, we couldn't help but look out at the breathtaking city view ahead of us. The joys on their faces were a testament to the deep appreciation they felt for all that had been done for them by their beloved mother.

After finishing a satisfying meal, we returned to our peaceful accommodation to a rest. Our purpose for sleeping early was to ensure we were well-rested and prepared for the forthcoming adventure that awaited us at Disneyland, a world-renowned for its wonders and captivating attractions.

After we had all woken up, we took showers and got ready for the excitement that was going to take place on this incredibly significant day for us....yay! We exited across the street and made our way to the shuttle stop to be transported to the theme park. We were in a long waiting queue for about 45 minutes. However, as we were brought to the front of the queue, we were instructed to board a shuttle bus that was either down the road or across the street since it would take too long for all of us to walk in that heat. When we came to the park and got in the queue to present our wristbands for the brace band system. So that the children might go on adventures. They were thrilled, especially considering the fact that both of them had witnessed Mickey Mouse Saviour content. After that, the kids got what they wanted because my daughter bought it. Then, we started looking for rides to ride on. I also took some rides. When we took one of the rides, all of us were laughing at first because it did not seem scary but the rides suddenly gained speed, which shocked us all. This was one of the most scary rides of my life. I started thinking it was going to throw my butt off. Kids and I were praying for the ride to stop. When I thought it was over, it never stopped. It dropped down against my thoughts. I was about to start pulling off my hair to get out of this scary ride. But in the end, we actually enjoyed it. After a long time, I got to spend some relaxing time with my daughter and my grandchildren. The kids had a great time travelling to and leaving Arizona. We stopped to purchase some cinnamon sticks, walked around, and talked, and then stopped at a savior's store on the way home.

In addition, my daughter took a picture of herself and her child with Mickey Mouse in front of a gate where you are no longer able to get your picture made with the character. After that, we were getting ready to depart the theme park and board the shuttle bus to head back to the hotel before heading back home the following days; nonetheless, the grandkids had a great time at the park. Therefore, once the shuttle brought us to our destination, we looked for the truck and then make our way back across the street to the hotel suite that they had reserved for us. The kids entered the room and were still running around and had fun while maintaining their independence. Those two played till they were sleep, which was excellent, so when the morning sunrise wind blew, we all awakened, ready to drive back to Arizona to return home. It had been a long drive, but the fun was about to end. When we were riding down the highway, we were all silent as we headed back to Arizona. After reaching Arizona, I drove back to their home to drop them off, and then I drove my truck and SUV back to my home. Upon arriving home, the first thing I did was unpacking my stuff to get ready for the next day.

Chapter 9

Darrell's Medical Condition Severed

March 2022

Darrell's Injury Due to Pressure Sore

On **14 March, 2022**, I went to the Estrella Care Center to ask for my husband's discharge paper so that he will be able to come home and transportation van will drive him home instead of me. I was faced with further difficulties after resolving my case with the social worker with Estrella care center for my spouse's release from the care center. I was instructed to continue with my departure and follow the instructions after signing the discharge papers for my husband. The staff understood my position after I explained to them that I wouldn't be leaving until ride of my husband had arrived. I decided to stay at the care facility where Darrell was being contained after observing a man bring Darrell down the hall and near awaiting van. The driver pushed Darrell inside as I waited outside. At that moment, I told the driver that someone was waiting for Darrell to return to the house, and I walked away the guy in the van driven off with my husband. When he was dropped off at his destination, Darrell's wheelchair lacked a seatbelt. As soon as I arrived home, I learned of this. When I got home, I looked at the video from my camera and saw the caregiver buckling Darrell's seat belt in his wheelchair. The caregiver then went to check on Darrell in his room to make sure he was dried and clean. As soon as Darrell's clothing were taken off, it became clear that the Estrella Care Center had not given him the proper degree of care during his prior stay. I have address my spouse with many pressure sores on his lower extremities (privates), a noticeably swollen right knee, and an almost softball-sized right ankle that felt like it was packed with fluid when touched, Darrell was brought back to me. On the right side of his body, Darrell was unable to use any of his extremities. His right arm, which he had been using before being placed at Estrella, was not locked in place across his chest, but it was so tight that moving it would cause him a great deal of discomfort, based on the expressions on Darrell's face and the fact that he was grabbing with his left hand. Darrell was unable to move his right leg because it was tied down and flexed at an angle, preventing full blood circulation to the leg. Darrell could not even move his left leg, which was similarly restrained. When Darrell was examined once more, the carer discovered numerous bruises on his right leg, buttocks, and arm. She also noted the swelling in Darrell's right leg. The person caring for Darrell then saw that his skin was horribly filthy, overly dry, and peeled in an alarming way. She continued by saying that she thought Darrell could need medical attention because she felt what might be a blood clot in his leg. Her hypothesis was that a blood clot was responsible for the growth. I wasted little time in getting in touch with my primary care physician and scheduling a zoom visit. During the transition, he began to grasp the carer so tightly that it was obvious he was upset about something. After that, I questioned Darrell about his condition, whether anything had happened, and why he was so anxiously clinging on the carer. The next thing Darrell did was point to his wheelchair and the ground at the same time. His partner explained that he had fallen when I asked him what had happened. He uttered those words while shaking his head. The care provider then explained to the patient that since she was a mandated reporter, she had to document what she had just witnessed in the Generations System report as well as report it to her immediate supervisor because it might be a sign of abuse. The carer then made all the necessary calls to inform the business that a formal report with Community Care Licensing was need to be filed since it was possible that Darrell had been ignored or hurt before being sent home from the care facility. Darrell was instructed to visit the emergency hospital so that his blood clots could be investigated after seeing his primary care doctor. In the emergency room on **29 March, 2022**, it was determined that Darrell needed to be admitted because of blood clots in his right leg. He was therefore admitted to a hospital. His groins area and the area of his legs were covered in blood clots. On **30 March, 2022**, after midnight, Darrell was transported by ambulance to the Abrazo Hospital on the west campus, where he was subsequently admitted. On **31 March, 2022**, my husband was finally allowed to leave Abrazo Hospital so that he could go home.

Chapter 10

Therapeutic Treatment for Darrell – Diagnosis of Osteoporosis

"Trust yourself. You know more than you think you do."
~ Benjamin Spock

April 2022

Darell's Undergoing Diverse Therapies

I spent most of **April 2022** attempting to obtain my husband different therapy. Physical therapy, speech therapy, and having his ears checked and cleansed since they were constantly leaking wax were just a few of the treatments he received. Additionally, my husband showed evidence of abuse even after being admitted to the Estrella Care Center, so I felt obligated to look into the idea of hiring legal counsel on his behalf and did so in the end. Sadly, I was unable to locate anyone who could assist me in the majority of these places. When I finally had a reference, I contacted every company that had been suggested, but not a single one could offer Darrell in-home care. Throughout the month Darrell attended a number of appointments in May. Just two days after leaving the At Abrazo West Campus, on **2 May, 2022**, Darrell noticed a change in his blood pressure. The range of the difference between the smallest and biggest values was between 113/96 and 150/90.

May 2022

Darrell Diagnosed with Osteoporosis

Darrell visited Bayless Health Care in Avondale, Arizona, on **3 May, 2022**, when he reportedly received a diagnosis of osteoporosis and an injection to cure it. Darrell's right leg ailment made him more and more averse to the idea of moving as the month of May went on. This was evident by the fact that Darrell kept grabbing at his leg or your hand whenever they moved or were touched, as well as by the expression on his face. Darrell began receiving twice-weekly 30-minute sessions of in-home physical therapy on **11 May, 2022**, after meeting with a physical therapist doctor for an initial evaluation on **9 May, 2022** (as reported by his attorney). Up until **11 May, 2022**, this persisted. On the first day of his physical therapy session, Darrell was clearly in a significant lot of discomfort as he did the stretching exercises. Darrell did not enjoy that he was being pulled and stretched since he was so rigid because it ached. On or about **16 May, 2022**, I bought a soft foot brace for Darrell to wear at night as per the physical therapist's advice in order to help him learn how to keep his foot straight. Darrell started using a hand brace during the day to help him learn how to maintain his hand straight. By **17 May 2022**, Darrell's limbs had started to regain some flexibility thanks to his participation in physical therapy and range-of-motion exercises. Even as he continued to pedal his bike, Darrell was able to unwind the muscles in his right leg and foot. Darrell's nurse practitioner in **2022** anticipated that on 18 May of that year, he would be referred for an ear examination and cleaning, but that never happened. Because my husband and I had been through so much together this year, I decided that we needed a vacation for **21 May**, which was also his and our birthday. I asked a friend to help me book a room in Las Vegas because I'm not very good at researching places to go and it had been so long that I didn't really know where to start, so I made the spontaneous decision to go with my husband to Las Vegas to see the Motown Review. On his birthday, **21 May, 2022**, we got up early. He was excited when I told him we were going to Las Vegas this morning to attempt to make it in time to attend the Motown revue this evening. We weren't stopping because our reservations for a hotel room and tickets for the revue had already been made. It was a long drive, but I was okay with it because I had our clothes packed up the night before, and I had told my husband to go to sleep so we could get up in the morning and take this ride on the highway towards Vegas.

He was eager to be free once and for all, so I got him into the truck and put the wheelchair in the back of the truck, then I drove off with my husband in the car. On the way halfway to Las Vegas, we passed a truck stop where they served food. When I went to the loo, they were incredibly kind and asked me if I would want to move to the other side, where my husband and I would have some privacy. She then added, "Follow me, and I'll take you back there." Because everything was so clean, I was able to assist my husband there. She just wanted him to be at ease in the bathroom where no one would be staring at him, which I completely understood. It was really clean inside and very huge with everything in it. We then exited the loo and proceeded into the restaurant to have breakfast, where we sat for an hour to eat. After that, we continued driving towards Las Vegas, and when we arrived there, he was eager to leave our home. We proceeded to check out the room, which was different than what I had anticipated from the website but nonetheless provided us with a place to rest for the night. Since we didn't have much time to relax in our room and I was hungry, I suggested that we watch the motion review show while we ate. The show is only around the corner from the hotel. When we arrived, I was informed that the snack bar was closed due to a restaurant remodel. I retorted that I did not have access to internet information, but I didn't want to ruin my husband's fun, so we waited until the door opened so that we could enter and see the Motown review. The person who let us in asked where we were from when we said we were from Arizona for my husband's birthday. When I replied that we were there to celebrate his birthday and see a show, he complimented me on taking my husband out because few people do that anymore due to his disability. I replied that it wasn't in my nature to care for a loved one before he became ill. My spouse was rocking to the music and had his eyelids up while we enjoyed the event. Supreme had me dancing to some music that I had not heard in a long. We loved spending time together as just the two of us after the performance. After the play, we went out to eat before going to bed. When we returned to our room, my husband Darrell settled in and went out.

He is currently enjoying himself. We're leaving in the morning, so I'd better get some rest so I can drive back to Arizona in the morning. Now that morning has arrived, we have cleaned up, brushed our teeth, dressed, and are ready to go. We travelled for four hours straight after leaving, and although I was exhausted, I still enjoyed having my spouse by my side. My husband was returned home, although he seemed to enjoy the chance to spend some time away from the house. On **24 May, 2022**, Darrell started experimenting with his voice to accomplish new things. Darrell was screaming obscenities at the caretaker in front of everyone, but it was thrilling to hear him talk. I quickly started making the appropriate phone calls in an attempt to reschedule speech treatment, but my efforts eventually proved unsuccessful. Darrell met with his nurse practitioner numerous times to discuss speech therapy, but he never started the procedure. Darrell started using the prescribed walker on **25 May** with the help of the physical therapist and the care provider. Due to his ability to take a total of three steps during this time, Darrell was able to successfully complete a significant number of steps. Darrell did not have much confidence in the walker, so he preferred to hold onto someone's shoulder before attempting to move forward. The physical therapist told me that Darrell would benefit most from wearing a soft boot on his foot for a few hours each day throughout the week to help him keep his right foot straight while going about his daily activities after his physical therapy session on **31 May, 2022**. Darrell continued his physical therapy sessions throughout the entire month of May, and by 1 June, he was visibly more flexible than before. Darrell had even managed to stop complaining about the pain he was feeling while performing his range-of-motion exercises, which was amazing to watch. Darrell continued to have gum irritation symptoms as of **3 June, 2022**. He kept poking his gums, and eventually they started to bleed.

Chapter 11

Life Challenges Continued

"Only the harshest personal experiences open our eyes to the immaculate possibilities and the splendor of our world."
~ **Kilroy J. Oldster**

June 2022

Letter from United Health Insurance

I received a letter on **6 June, 2022**,

charging me for my husband's injuries sustained on **31 December, 2021**.

The moment I became aware that my inner anxieties were on the verge of materializing. I failed to comprehend the reasoning behind United Health Insurance's decision to issue a bill to me. Nevertheless, they proceeded to do so. Upon presenting the letter to my healthcare provider with the intention of gaining a better understanding of its contents, my care provider duly noted that my spouse was not under my direct supervision at the moment when the injury in question was caused. The care provider thereafter recommended that I furnish a duplicate of the aforementioned letter to the legal representative of my spouse and inform her of the fact that Darrell and I possess supporting evidence about an incident that transpired when Darrell was being looked after by Estrella Care Center, as Mable had mentioned to authorities.

June 2022

Darrell's Treatment

Due to the high secretion of wax from Darrell's ears, his nurse practitioner was once again contacted to explore the potential of scheduling an ear-cleaning procedure on **8 June, 2022**. This action was undertaken in an attempt to rectify the problem at hand. The following three days of Darrell's physical treatment, commencing on **14 June** and extending through **17 June, 2022**, proceeded as planned. Darrell exhibited physical signs of distress as he tightly grasped his chair, while providing minimal verbal responses in the form of affirmative murmurs to the questions posed by the physical therapist regarding his current state of health.

Darrell consistently adhered to his regular appointment routine. Nevertheless, on **15 June, 2022,** he was accompanied to Arizona Oncology for a medical consultation, during which a total of 15 blood samples were collected for a diverse range of diagnostic examinations. The visit was arranged to occur at Arizona Oncology. Unfortunately, it came to my knowledge on **16 June, 2022,** that the laboratory worker had made a mistake in handling all 15 blood tubes.

Consequently, Darrell was compelled to revisit Arizona Oncology on the subsequent day, **17 June, 2022,** in order to undergo a second round of blood collection and additional testing for all 15 vials. My husband experienced fatigue and irritability as a result of this situation over the following two days. Due to the caregiver's inability to facilitate Darrell's showering, she turned to administering bed baths on the occasions when he was capable of showering.

This was done to keep Darrell from getting dizzy and losing his balance. On **21 June, 2022**, Darrell's physical therapist communicated to me that he would get benefits from supplementary physical therapy sessions that might be conducted in a home setting. On **23 June, 2022**, a meeting took place with the physical therapist responsible for Darrell's treatment. It was determined during this conversation that Darrell would be able to proceed with his physical therapy. Upon initially receiving this information, I experienced an overwhelming sense of pleasure. Subsequently, Darrell proceeded with his treatment plan at the physical therapist's facility for an additional duration of two weeks. Darrell commenced his second round of physical therapy on **29 June, 2022**. The objective of this session was to further enhance the muscular and articular structures in Darrell's right upper extremity and lower extremity. Presently, Darrell is engaged in efforts to enhance the muscular endurance and stability of his core muscles in order to maximize the use of his upper body strength.

Chapter 12

Life Gave Some Reasons to Smile

"A song and a smile from someone I cared about could be enough to distract me from all that darkness, if only for a little while."
~ **Ransom Riggs**

July 2022

Improvement in Darrell's Medical

Condition

Darrell's consistent adherence to a prescribed physical treatment regimen facilitated significant improvements in his condition. Darrell was surprised to discover that he wasn't feeling any of the pain he often did while performing this exercise as he was now lying on his stomach to stretch. Darrell initiated manual pedaling of his exercise bike in order to alleviate stiffness in his right shoulder and elbow area. On **1 July, 2022**, Darrell initiated the activity of pushing his medicine ball in multiple directions and engaged in diverse methods to make contact with or grab it. Around **6 July, 2022**, Darrell started providing assistance to the caretaker by accompanying them in the shower to facilitate the process of bathing, subsequent drying, and the dressing. This generated an immense amount of joy for me as it represented an important achievement for Darrell. On **11 July , 2022,** Darrell began taking a higher dosage of his medication, levetiracetam. Regrettably, this resulted in a state of sluggishness and lethargy for him, to the extent that his ability to engage in physical therapy was compromised.

At a certain point, Darrell was informed that he would undergo an assessment to determine his eligibility for receiving a suitable wheelchair on **12 July, 2022**. Based on the assessment conducted by Darrell's physical therapist, it was determined that the current wheelchair being utilized by Darrell is considered unsuitable. In order to accommodate Darrell's body, it was essential to extend and raise the wheelchair. After engaging in a conversation with Darrell's Nurse Practitioner, it was mutually agreed upon that she would undertake the responsibility of initiating the referral process for either replacement wheelchair components or entirely new components. During a significant portion of **July 2022,** Darrell's outstanding achievements were prominently showcased. In the month of July, Darrell exhibited independent vertical movement, implying an increase in upper body strength as a result of the recent implementation of prone stretching activities. Darrell had been performing these exercises in a prone position. Even though Darrell was making good progress, he was still having trouble receiving any form of aid with various medical, dental, and rehabilitation services.

Despite Darrell's notable advancements, he encountered persistent challenges in obtaining any form of assistance. Darrell sought a consultation with an otolaryngologist at Estrella on **15 July, 2022**, with the goal of undergoing an evaluation to ascertain the necessity of speech therapy. Nevertheless, he was not recommended for speech therapy. In spite of my husband's sincere efforts to engage in communication with both myself and others, I encountered many justifications for my inability to arrange speech therapy sessions for him, regardless of the frequency of my attempts to contact the relevant parties or the number of times I was instructed to follow up. The dental procedure that Darrell required on **18 July, 2022** presented an additional challenge for our team. After a manual inspection at the Smile dental clinic, I was informed that Darrell would need to be evaluated at a facility that specialized in treating people with specific needs. Darrell was transported to the Smile dental office. I was provided with an additional clarification that in order to do the requisite surgical procedures, it would be imperative to provide anesthesia to Darrell, inducing a state of unconsciousness for the entirety of the operation. Darrell received regular follow-up treatment from his home-based physical therapist and his doctor, who specializes in physical therapy. The happening of this event ultimately proved to be a beneficial outcome. During his meeting with his physical therapist on **20 July, 2022**, Darrell effectively demonstrated the progress being made through both verbal and physical means while also articulating his emotional state at the time.

Chapter 13

Life Is Still Testing Darrell and Me

"Every day you are being tested that's just life."
           ~ **Alburtis Turner**

21 July 2022

Drowsiness and Visual Blurriness Issues

On **21 July, 2022**, despite Darrell's engagement in physical therapy, there was an observable disparity in his physical state compared to his previous condition. Darrell displayed indications of drowsiness and appeared to have visual blurriness. Upon seeing these indicators, the physical therapist and the carer reached the decision to postpone the initiation of physical therapy. Both individuals proceeded to assess Darrell's blood pressure, and upon doing so, they ascertained that it was elevated. The blood pressure of the individual was assessed using both manual and electronic means, utilizing two distinct blood pressure equipment. In all three instances, the recorded results were observed to be significantly elevated. Additionally, his blood pressure exhibited a significantly increased level.

Despite my absence from home, the carer promptly informed me about my husband's condition, prompting me to quickly return. When I informed the nurse practitioner, Darrell, about his ailment, she recommended administering the prescribed prescription for managing his high blood pressure. I was required to provide it to him anytime his blood pressure exceeded the prescribed threshold. Subsequently, Darrell received care in accordance with her instructions. I diligently monitored Darrell's condition, along with the other carer, until his blood pressure was restored to its normal level. As of **22 July, 2022**, Darrell's blood pressure has reached a state of stability. On **23 July, 2022** she left out my home because she was with me at doctor's office.

Although being fully aware of the fact that Darrell's requirements would be adequately attended to in her absence, the caretaker of Darrell made the regrettable decision to embark on a vacation at the conclusion of **July 2022**.

The designated individuals for replacement failed to start their job with Darrell, and no attempts were made to establish communication with me, so placing me in a dilemma. This means that after undergoing hand surgery, I was nevertheless obliged to physically lift my spouse while being mindful of not unintentionally dropping him, ignorant to the discomfort I was enduring as a result of the surgical procedure.

. Despite the communication I had with Darrell, a nurse practitioner, when he indicated that there was no immediate need for me to seek medical attention until Thursday, **2 August, 2022**, it is noteworthy that Darrell's blood pressure remained high for the entirety of the day. Subsequently, Darrell underwent a series of x-ray examinations, during which it was ascertained that sedation was necessary for him to undergo hospital-based x-ray procedures including the administration of contrast dye by injection. As a consequence, it became imperative for Darrell to undergo radiographic imaging at the medical facility. Subsequently, Darrell's blood pressure became unmanageable, necessitating his transfer to the hospital by emergency staff. Over the next few days, there was a persistent pattern of changing blood pressure readings in Darrell. The healthcare professional and I conducted continuous monitoring of Darrell's vital signs, including temperature, pulse, and blood pressure, until a subsequent fall in his blood pressure was observed.

August 2022

A close check on Darrell

During the entire month of August, we closely monitored all three of these crucial indicators. Due to Darrell's blood pressure condition, a series of cardiac ultrasounds were scheduled as a precautionary measure to ascertain the absence of any hidden medical conditions that may have been disregarded. The previously mentioned tests were scheduled ahead of time. Darrell reported a significant improvement in his condition on **8 August, 2022**. On **9 August, 2022**, Darrell made a subsequent endeavor to establish contact with the physical therapist. Darrell sought medical attention on **11 August, 2022**, in order to undergo a follow-up assessment of his blood clots and to undergo an examination of his neck to ascertain the underlying cause of his impaired ability to keep an erect head posture. Darrell diligently attended all of the appointments listed on his schedule. On **15 August, 2022**. Darrell initiated the process of dressing himself and promptly immersed himself in his physical therapy regimen upon commencing self-assistance. Darrell adhered to the instructions provided by the physical therapist on **17 August**

2022, by recommencing the activity of kicking the medicine ball and performing overhead reaches, with the objective of establishing contact with or grasping the ball. On **22 August 2022**, the carer and I devoted a significant amount of our focus to remembering Darrell. I made the effort to locate and procure a collection of old images and home videos with the intention of presenting them to Darrell.

Darrell's capacity to recall specific

details and individuals from the video and photographs was acknowledged by his affirmative gestures and responses, which were accompanied by smiles and nods of agreement. On **23 August, 2022**, Darrell initiated a new cycle of physical therapy involving the utilization of a medicine ball. Throughout the entirety of the session, he demonstrated exceptional performance. Furthermore, the individual underwent a neck massage to facilitate muscular elongation and maybe induce a state of relaxation. Initially, he exhibited a lack of enthusiasm for undergoing physical treatment; however, he swiftly developed a positive attitude towards it. On **24 August, 2022**, my spouse had a notably sad demeanor, experiencing intermittent periods of depression on several occasions. My spouse encountered challenges in adapting to the new circumstances. However, as of

25 August, 2022, the individual began exhibiting improved mobility within the bed, demonstrating enhanced utilization of both limb and core musculature. Since the commencement of their professional relationship on **14 March, 2022**, my spouse has benefited from the unwavering assistance and advocacy provided by their care provider. As a result of her caregiver influence, he has consistently had a sense of ease and peace in her company, while she has played a pivotal role in ensuring his adherence to his daily routine. She assumed the role of holding him responsible for the execution of the tasks assigned to him on a daily basis.

On **29 August, 2022**, an assessment was conducted on the wheelchair utilized by my spouse, which was deemed more suitable for a youngster of 12 years of age, to explore potential alternatives for its replacement. At the given moment, the individual in question had reached the age of 60, and a sense of elation permeated our collective being with the arrival of the technician responsible for the provision of the wheelchair. Following the departure of the other individual, Darrell, the caretaker, and I reclined, partaking in the seeing of a film while consuming popcorn, all while maintaining a steadfast conviction that Darrell's circumstances will improve after the restoration of the chair.

Obtaining the appropriate equipment might pose significant challenges when individuals are constrained by a low budget and must depend on Medicare for the provision of wheelchair parts. On the morning of **30 August, 2022**, my spouse successfully achieved an upright position within the shower enclosure, aided by the presence of a grab bar, which was utilized for additional stability and support. I fortuitously encountered an instance wherein the carer expressed gratitude towards a divine being. Consequently, I promptly approached him, who was in an upright position with his lower limbs extended and his feet firmly positioned on the ground.

Chapter 14

Happy Days Were Just Knocking

"Love is that condition in which the happiness of another person is essential to your own."
                    ~ Anonymous

September 2022

Remarkable improvement in Darrell's condition

My husband exhibited remarkable walking ability while sitting in his chair. He did an excellent job of moving from his chair to the patio window that day. The caretaker and the physical therapist were taking him ahead, and I was thrilled to see them do so with further support. He was also able to say yes when it was appropriate, and not the other way around on that day.

On **2 September, 2022,** Darrell was doing extremely well. He recently had a meeting with his physician, and he was then using a cardiac monitor that was installed in his bed by a separate firm. It was only possible to remove this monitor for a total of two hours during the whole day, which was about 24 hours till September 16th of that year.

My husband used to sleep most of the time during the day since he felt very exhausted after his session with the physician followed by lunch.

It could be better if he improved his communication with the physical therapist and the care provider.

My husband had a good day on **5 September 2022** and appreciated the special lunch that was provided to him. He also did very well with the caregiver who assisted him in putting on his clothing during the day.

When my husband went to get his blood drawn on **7 September 2022**, the needle used was a butterfly needle, but he had a difficult time throughout the process at the laboratory.

The technician drew fifteen tubes of blood, and then my care provider, who was assisting my husband with his daily routine, went down the elevator and received a phone call saying that we had performed the incorrect procedure.

As a result, I was going to have to accompany my husband back to the laboratory. Thank God, they did not make an incorrect diagnosis on him and expressed a willingness to try again. Due to the phone call, we were waiting for the van to get us up so that we could return to my residence.

On September 13, 2022 my hubby was in good health those days. His assistance with transitions and showering continued throughout the day. Darrell had understood that he would be receiving cardiac monitoring and that he had to wait until **15 September 2022**, at noon, for it to be removed. However, he would not be required to travel with me because I could bring the equipment back.

During the early hours of the morning of **15 September 2022**, my husband was quite animated, and the caregiver was playing music for Darrell, which was Darrell's favorite instrument. As the music rocked to the beat, my husband started to sing the song's lyrics. At that time, this was a huge step toward getting Darrell speech therapy, and he was thrilled to be able to express as many words as he could.

Additionally, during the morning, he participated in physical therapy and did well in standing up on two feet. He also performed exceptionally while moving from the room to the family room as I cheered for him.

Darrell and I went out on the town in Glendale, Arizona, later in the evening. We all expressed our support for him as he proceeded on his path to success.

As time went on, we continued to strongly encourage and assist him. When we went out for dinner to celebrate my birthday, I felt he was looking fantastic. I had a few drinks, relaxed, and talked to him while he listened to me attentively. He looked across the room to see others around us. I believed he was having a wonderful time.

On 16 September 2022 Darrell made a lot of effort to apply his full body pressure on both legs when he was participating in physical therapy. We realized that Darrell would soon begin actively participating in some kind of speech treatment too.

Darrell was behaving very positively on **19 September 2022** and seemed to be very happy and relaxed. He took heavy breakfast and lunch, sat and spent time staring at the garden, and just took a nap for an hour. Darrell was quite enthusiastic and active in those days.

By 20 September 2022, Darrell has made a great deal of improvement since beginning his step physical therapy. As he continued to make an effort to walk, he also started eating well.

According to the results of various tests that were performed today recently, Darrell was putting on weight, and his skin appeared to be in good condition.

On 21 September 2022, Darrell relied on standing assistance; he took a step and stayed there for roughly seven minutes. When Darrell finished his dinner, he went outside to look at the range, and then he went to sleep.

Although Darrell was a bit reluctant on 22 **September 2022,** he participated in physical therapy and did quite well moving forward with the steps. He could move from the living room to the kitchen and back twice with the support of the assistant.

On 23 September 2022, Darrell had a truly remarkable day. I was so much emotional and thrilled when the caregiver told me that during the transition from the wheelchair to the shower, he stretched out to grip the bar, and then managed to get up himself without any help, on both legs, with both feet planted firmly on the ground. Because my husband refused to sit down, he stood up for a period of five minutes without any help, and the caregiver said that it was an amazing sight to see.

Additionally, Darrell continued making progress to regain his ability to walk and to use his right arm. Moreover, he extended his finger in the same manner. Along with its ability to move his right leg and toe without help, Darrell was also able to repair transition assistance.

He was making every possible effort to resume walking. At the same time, he was trying hard to communicate.

On 28 September, 2022 I showed the caregiver a movie that we shot when the children were younger presenting how much Darrell loved teaching his children all about skiing. My husband seemed to take pleasure in the period of his life in which everything appeared to be functioning normally.

When he was able to communicate, the caregiver could also see him and engage with his children and family; Darrell looked to want me to go back in time with those great experiences back to him; it was encouraging to see how interested he was in the past.

All this accomplished for him this afternoon was to help him recall how to walk, communicate, and eat his food. He was smiling most of the time.

Chapter 15

Hard Time Finding a Reliable Therapy Service

Never give up, and be confident in what you do. There may be tough times, but the difficulties which you face will make you more determined to achieve your objectives and to win against all the odds."
~ Marta

October 2022

Tried hard to find physical therapy services for Darrell

My husband's caretaker and I practiced physical therapy on him to assist in strengthening his arms and legs and to loosen up his limbs. His final physical therapy appointment was on **4 October, 2022**, but as of today, he continued to attend sessions and performed really well. He moved from the kitchen counter to a sliding glass door and helped himself by bending both legs and balancing himself. He also stood for four minutes that day in his lift chair with assistance from both his legs and feet.

We were also working on using a voice-activated technological gadget to assist with word recognition and attempting to whisper at the moment.

Though he was beginning to start understanding it, progress was quite slow. He had started to learn how to use the gadget, but we also needed to make sure he understood that, despite the vibration and sound it produced.

I had scheduled Darrell's appointment with a nurse practitioner on 7 October 2022, hoping to receive a referral for physical therapy. However, she declined to provide services because I was not willing to provide her with information about physical therapy that would end; I told her that I couldn't provide that information until I had a conversation with an attorney regarding my husband's case.

On 28 October 2022, my Best Friend Diane and Phillip stopped by to see me and my husband after their birthday. I was delighted to have them both see us on their way back to California. The following day, when it was still light, I gave her a tour of my garden and she conducted a culinary tasting using some of my favorite spices. I offered her to take whatever they would like to take home with them.

In addition, my dad received a visit from Diane and Phillips, and he was overjoyed to see them. As people age, some things do brighten their day.

My friend stopped by to meet my daughter and my grandchildren on **29 October, 2022**. After seeing them, she left to return to California, but we were glad she had made the trip because she had traveled through sunny Arizona.

November 2022

My Aunt's Death

My dad was unhappy to lose his sister on **3 November 2022,** since my aunt died before his birthday. The last time we saw her was on 20 June 2022, which was also her birthday, and she seemed to like us all.

You never know when God is going to call you home, so cherish your time with your parents while they are still here. Once your eyes close, you will never be able to tell them how much you love them. I am happy I got to spend some time with my aunt; we worked out our differences while she was still alive.

December 2022

Searching for a New Physician

We had my aunt's memorial service on **4 December 2022,** at her church. After everything was said and done, I had to start working on getting my husband to find someone for physical therapy. After that, I began interacting with the doctor in the next week. I contacted the practician nurse and offered to provide her the phone for the attorney so she could contact him and inquire what information she needed, but she continued to refuse to call on her own.

The lady was a caretaker; she behaved ghetto in my house, acting as though she was about to harm me. I had the impression that I was residing in Oakland, California. Although you are providing services for my spouse in my home, I strive to act professionally and with respect even if I might take it to the street. Then she departed, saying that if you don't trust her She chose to leave my house, so I didn't stop her. I just said "Goodbye".

Then, I made the decision to switch to a new physician instead of a practitioner who can assist Darrell with certain areas of physical therapy, physical occupational therapy, and speech; however, Darrell and I won't be able to visit the new physician until 14

December, 2022. He began working with Darrell, and I was quite happy. To help Darrell get back on track, he sent a recommendation for speech and physical therapy.

January 2023

Darrell's Physical Therapy at Home

On **2 January 2023,** Darrell started home physical treatment with the provider.

On **9 January 2023,** I called to arrange for an evaluation at my residence so that he could get services from physical therapy in my home. It was a successful day. She admitted that it was difficult for her to get my husband in and out of chair and onto his feet. So, she said she would try for a bit to see how it went, but she did not want to break her back. We had to keep working on him every day to keep the limb free, so when the woman arrived at my house, she stretched her limbs out on the right side where it was tight. Additionally, the leg that was tight maintained the limbs moving appropriately.

Darrell had an appointment on **27 January 2023,** for new wheelchair parts at 2:00. His armrest was causing his arm to bend at the wrist, and he was just too tall for the wheelchair. He was thus receiving additional components to make the wheelchair fit his height—he is at least 5'9."

My spouse was informed it would take two to three hours to fix the chair, so the caretaker and I waited while it got fixed. After that, we placed my husband to sleep on the bed that was in there so he could relax.

Once they completed the repairs, I was overjoyed that my husband's legs could again be relaxed to the proper length for his height in a wheelchair.

February 2023

The Caregiver Left

The woman said that working with Darrell was too difficult and that she could no longer do it. Since neither of us was a physical therapist, we were again on our own, attempting to find out how to deal with Darrell in that capacity. We therefore began walking using the aid that we had been provided following therapeutic instruction.

In terms of speaking, we just had daily conversations with him as normal people do since we were not speech therapist. I was unable to locate anyone in the city of Buckeye, Arizona, who would come to the house after that firm left.

There wasn't a lot of activity until February ended.

April 2023

Darrell Performed Several Tests for Kidneys

On **19 April 2023,** Darrell went for some routine tests to monitor the performance of his kidney, which is examined every six months.

At 2:45 p.m., on **29 April, 2023** he

scheduled an appointment with the kidney doctor. According to the doctor, A part of his kidney was not performing well, but otherwise, he was ok, with a kidney function of 62%.

Chapter 16

Watching Your Love Smiling is Best Ever Feeling

Love means to see the one you love happy."
  ~ **Nicholas Sparks**

May 2023

Darrell's Birthday Celebrations

On 5 May 2023, I brought Darrell to the Barbar shop to get his birthday hair done.

As an early birthday present, I took him to see The Whisper on Sunday, **14 May** in Chandler, Arizona. We also spent one night at the Gila Vee Casino Hotel.

After the show, I took him to the casino area so he could play the slots. He played for about an hour until he reached $250.00, at which point it was time to stop. Following that, we headed to our hotel in order to get some rest.

On **15 May 2023**, upon waking up on Monday I took a moment to lie down and stare at my spouse. Although he was mute, he might not realize how fortunate he was to still have me in his life.

Some ladies and families may pass him by without realizing the nonverbal nature of his stroke. As his spouse, I did the right thing and was at his side during good times and bad.

My concerns about leaving eventually vanished, and I got out of bed to take a shower in preparation for taking Darrell and myself home. After getting my spouse dressed, I will be prepared to exit the Gila River Hotel Casino.

I immediately made a call to the ballet to have my car transported to the hotel, and I contacted the bellman to come to collect our bag. After Bell Man arrived, we all departed and rode the elevator to my truck, where we were met by the valet parking guy. Because the bellman handled our luggage and loaded my car so efficiently, we tipped both of them for their excellent work.

My spouse and I had lot of fun. Thus, we set off when we were in the truck returning home from a little trip that included visiting our niece.

We really wanted to make a trip to

California in the **mid of May** and meet our niece but this could not happen since Darrell had so many appointments. Finally, we cancelled the trip.

A few months prior, he had made an appointment with the doctor, but was unable to see him because, after trying to draw his blood multiple times, his confidence broke. He said, "I can do it as often as I want," but I told him that he might lead my husband to death, which he was not feeling at all, so he stopped.

Chapter 17

There were Still Some Challenges

Every challenge you face today makes you stronger tomorrow. The challenge of life is intended to make you better, not bitter."
            ~ Roy T. Bennett

June 2023

Facing Lots of Challenges During Darrell's Treatment

In the meantime, I had to return with my husband on 21 June. When I visited the front desk employee was very rude to me and yelled at me without a reason when I asked where I needed to fill out the paperwork. She didn't know why she was making such a fuss when Darrell had an appointment and front desk let everyone be seen before Darrell. I waited patiently until he was called back to see the physician.

His appointment was at 9 am but he was seen at 10:45 am. We arrived at the back room and waited for the medical assistant to take our blood pressure before the doctor arrived. He was accompanied by a strange woman who asked him questions about the number of blood clots that had been diagnosed and that he would need to take blood thinners for the rest of his life. He had never experienced this before entering a care facility. When he emerged, clots were growing up and pressing against his heart; he was dehydrated and wanted to hide from the staff because I had given him excellent care at home.

He could have died if I had left him there any longer. When you are unable to speak and you require their assistance to support your medical staff, the system is just broken. How the system handles people saddens me much, especially when it comes to a handicapped person who is completely unable to advocate for themselves nonverbally.

The next day, I got a letter from the attorney's office saying that there was nothing wrong with him and that he wasn't wounded, but when he got home, he had all kinds of bedsores and they were afraid to go after them. I will not recommend this legal office to anybody.

They did not know how to handle a neglect case. They only knew how to deal with a case involving a vehicle accident, thus it took them nearly 18 months to find someone else to take up the case. After hearing that I should move quickly to locate another lawyer who has handled cases similar to this one, I took a seat back and considered the uncertainty I had been subjected to over the mistreatment done to my spouse.

Despite this, I would not give up. I hope that something can be done so that those who work in these facilities are held responsible for their conduct rather than merely given a pat on the back while people's health declines. Putting a family member in the cemetery—which I referred to as the "care center not protective at all"—is dangerous. During all of this, a caregiver jumped up and left. I asked her if she had seen anything in my house, and she replied that she hadn't.

The mess between us continued, so she jumped up and left again, but not before getting in my face and trying to talk trash. She was the type to spread rumors about others, saying nonsense into discussions as she entered your home. She was talking to me without knowing what she was saying. The caregiver was extremely timid when it came to posing a personal question to me. I look at her thinking about who I let in my home. I am very thankful God sent a person that is just about her job not about my business .I am grateful that

I pray I do not deal with mess like this no more, or Lord please take me home so that I don't have to suffer like my husband is right now people in and out of your home and the loss of your family will sting like a salad bar without assistance.

I am relieved that the disgusting, ugly woman is no longer my husband caregiver so she no longer has to come to my house.

July 2023

Shifting to a New Law Firm

I discovered another law firm on 14 July and they accepted my case to see if their firm could help me with my lawsuit so that my husband might receive fair treatment.

This was my final attempt to fight the company that screwed my husband up. As a result, we were waiting to hear from the top law firm that specialized in cases of this kind of negligence. The patient arrived home with extremely dry skin, was severely dehydrated, and drank five glasses of water in the hopes that something could be done.

The doctor wants to tell us that he has always been this way, which is untrue; he was working against his patients and was unable to speak to us face-to-face because he was lying to us about my husband's medical records.

We felt at that point that he was the real devil, questioning like a urologist or doctor, so we left him there with little hope for the future. I started searching for another urological doctor who cared about their patients and wasn't simply in it for the money as soon as I got home.

With the assistance of the insurance company, I was able to locate another physician in our network who specializes in kidney blood clots and can provide more bedside care. It is less likely that those with darker complexion would receive subpar care from these professionals, who are beginning to voice their opinions about the health care system.

In nursing homes nationwide, more than 47.8 million people are being neglected. Presently, stroke patients who have experienced tremendous trauma and are mute owing to nonverbal communication are frequently abused and neglected. This is partly because stroke patients and personnel are burnt out. 64.2% of nursing home employees admitted to abusing patients in some way.

A very terrible situation to be in when you are unable to take care of yourself and feel uncared for, especially if no family sees their loved one sometimes. The client returns home with bedsores, dehydrated skin, cracking pealing, and malnutrition.

I have no doubt in my mind that my spouse has been neglected, and that his case would have been handled much more successfully if he had been white.

I'm so sick of the unjust way the current system is set up for when someone is harmed and nobody can help them.

I suggest that people only go into a care center if they are dying, and even then, I would scream if I had to walk in there with an ice cream cone.

Please, before you send your love ones in there, please, take my word for it and look into it before heading down that path.

Chapter 18
Some Relaxing Time

"Sometimes the most productive thing you can do is relax."

~ **Mark Black**

September 2023

My Birthday Celebrations

My birthday is on 15th September. I was getting ready for it. We went to a Benihana restaurant in September, and although the food was good, my husband did not like it at all. We left, thinking that I would be able to go out later because he would be staying with a caregiver.

As a result, I was able to go out at

2:30 PM to the desert casino in Glendale, Arizona. I arrived, parked my SUV truck in the garage, got out, and rode the elevator to the first floor, where the casino was located.

I got a glass of wine and sat down, watching people gamble and all the happy faces I saw. Sometimes it's nice to go somewhere by yourself, and I was excited to be there by myself, talking to the people who were seated. It was very relaxing to watch so many people. I didn't win anything from my little gaming, but I did feel like a winner when I first walked in, especially on my birthday. That being said, I didn't go overboard and play any machines at all. I thus departed at almost nine o'clock at night and returned home.

He stated that I may go outside three or four times when I return home to take over as his caretaker. Despite my inability to comprehend what he had just stated three times, I was relieved that he was expressing himself clearly. I questioned him why he had done that because I had left you here and had not gotten you to go with me on my birthday, and he had continued to chuckle.

That night, as I sat with him, he continued to speak to me in a normal manner. I smiled at him and told him that you needed to talk to me and exhibit emotion all the time. I wished him a good night's kiss and said that I hoped to see him again tomorrow when I woke up.

I have no fascinating things to say about this month since I don't have my grandchildren around, so it was really quiet. However, I started talking to my cousin because she was organizing my dad's 90th birthday and she was inviting my husband to attend.

Chapter 19

Although Unpleasant but Some Relations Persists

"... bad memories always seem to have a way of being remembered over the good."

~ Jennifer L. Armentrout

October 2023

<u>Memories of my Bitter Relationship with my Dad</u>

At first, I was uncomfortable going to the gathering with the family I was very uneasy so I had no interest in going to his birthday.

My dad wanted all the attention, saying that my kids loved him more than me and my daughter did not care about me because we hadn't spoken to each other.

My dad never liked my husband at all, and I allowed him to live with us for three years, which was terrible. He destroyed my big screen TV, which I had for twenty-five years, and I found the old TV, maybe an eight-inch screen TV in the garage. He plugged it up and refused to buy a TV. He always said that my mother forced him to pay child support and that she did not want him anymore, therefore I never wanted to hear that kind of conversation I was a child then but as adult, he continues to bring it up.

Regretfully, I was relieved that he left my house because he was the reason my husband's blood pressure stayed high and I nearly suffered a heart attack. His style of thinking is the explanation for all these reasons why I did not want to go.

November 2023

My Dad's Birthday and Thanksgiving

Day Celebrations

On 5 November 2023, my cousin—who had thrown my dad's party—told me that there wouldn't be enough food if I brought my husband and a friend. After all that chaos, I discovered that she was expecting us to arrive alone so she could lock my husband and me in a room with my daughter and my dad because we weren't talking to each other.

As embarrassing as it may be, my husband and I went to church despite how uneasy it was. However, being the woman that I am, I refused to allow anybody to put me in danger, so my husband and I sat down next to my father, who waved for us to join him, along with my friend Susan.

I had witnessed this previously; a niece of his had followed his lead and went along with everything he said. Later in the service, when everyone was having a good time, he asked if I had seen the twins, to which I replied that I had, and as soon as I got to the door, your pastor was waiting outside for some reason to let us into the church. I entered so he could humiliate me as a daughter of his at this church as I did not understand it.

I guess my dad was supposed to be dancing, but I was surprised that he played the part of being unbalanced and unable to lift his leg, so he needed his walker to help him stay on his feet and bring enough food to bring my friend.

If I had not made it back to the church, I would not have seen the lied as well. He was supposed to be a dad but couldn't keep the family together but rather keep us apart. He was supposed to be a Christian and as older man, so he should have known better than to play dirty tricks on my husband and me.

My husband also couldn't speak or express himself to my dad, so this lady I seen the next day in the store was ashamed of being identified as a

Christian a pastor at that she was shame. I wanted my husband to get out of this box and speak because he knows all those people have done him wrong also, and this was a tremendous trick to play on anyone. It's your family that not supposed to mistreat like a nursing homes.

Because of the way he treated me, I'm not sure whether he is my father. I'm relieved that day was done because I needed to give God and this insane man something to think about and let go of on **5 November 2023.**

My Dad had a family member call him, but he pretended to be too busy to say thank you. He was very ungrateful that was his son and granddaughter called him on his 90th birthday whom he did not wish to get on the phone. He was very excited to have people around him on his birthday he was overwhelmed, at the party after everyone ate dinner folk started to help clean up the church kitchen and see who wanted to bring food back home. Then all begin to head to our care to go back home, I was going to transport my dad asks where will I put his walker he did not want to leave it because I did not have room in my truck his niece said do not worry I brought him to the church I can bring him back so me and my husband and a friend I got into to my truck and left.

To avoid having to spend Thanksgiving Day with my entire

family, I went to a friend's house on the day of Thanksgiving and celebrated with her and her spouse.

Darrell loved the journey to and from their house; we were both glad my husband made light jokes with them, making him feel at ease and free from constant scrutiny. Even though I know it makes him unhappy, you can treat my husband like a man and not a child.

Despite this, my husband finds it difficult to express himself. When my spouse is having fun and wants to start a discussion, and everyone pays close attention, it makes us feel happy.

Darrell, then, had a pleasant Thanksgiving Day and hopes to have many more days like this over the winter.

Nothing would fulfill my roles as a wife and caretaker more than I would sacrifice my life for.

Chapter 20

Christmas and New Year – Life is Gaining Back Colors

"Christmas isn't a season. It's a feeling."

~ Edna Ferber

December 2023

Christmas and New Year Celebrations

Christmas is a huge month for my spouse, even if I don't celebrate it. However, I had to make sure he had fun, so we were invited to a friend from another city, who agreed to have us over for dinner. I prepare dinner cakes and pies for potluck.

We didn't go out often, so I didn't have to buy stuff for me to wear. Even though he couldn't speak, he could understand me when I started getting ready for Christmas and told him it was approaching on a certain date on the calendar.

On **25 December 2023, we** got ready

and headed across town to a friend's house that she had asked us to. After helping him get into the vehicle, I arranged everything else including gifts and my husband's table, which he had his own personal table ensure he be comfort while we were away from home.

When we got there, she was with a coworker and her brother. She therefore introduced me to a long-time colleague. We were fortunate to be asked out since it was pleasant for my spouse and I to interact with others rather than stay home and watch TV.

My spouse enjoyed this type of get-together since he was rather gregarious at home, and we joked around and exchanged gifts that we had given each other. We prepared to return home once our fun with our friend was over. I could see by the look on his face that Darrell was having fun, and that when we got home, he didn't want to stay up late with me.

We traveled across town on 31 December to ring on New Year's Eve along with some friends. 2024 will be an exciting year for me as I bring my new book to life and get it in front of as many people as possible.

Chapter 21

Narrowly Escaping a Scam

"You will find peace not by trying to escape your problems, but by confronting them courageously. You will find peace not in denial, but in victory."

~ J. Donald Walters

February 2024

Facebook Hacked and Fake Call Regarding My Daughter's Kidnapping

What happened that day: I wanted

to return my cell phone because it was giving me trouble, and it was hacked on Facebook. So I went to Metro PCs in the morning, where the woman was trying to replace the phone. She was unable to do so since my passcode would not function and it contained a man named Mike.

I eventually gave the main branch a call. I was informed that my phone was set to high security, which I never put on my phone. She continued, saying, "You are correct—the passcode belongs to you, but we need to change it."

After we had done that, she interacted with Metro PC phone services, and everything was resolved. Therefore, I was able to get the phone. Then, on Friday night I did not know anyone on my page—It was crazy I seen a woman who works for my husband—was on my friend list strange.

Since my page was not at all friendly, I declared on Monday that I would be returning this phone to the Metro PC phone. Thus, on Monday, 19 February 2024, I traveled back there in an attempt to retrieve my Facebook account.

As soon as I got out of the car, a phone call came in saying "This is Officer Mike on the phone. He said that my daughter was hurt in an accident. I also heard a voice like my daughter. I asked if she was hurt in the accident as she was crying. He said, "I have to go outside to talk because the Metro PC phone company is too noisy." I then went outside, and he threatened to chop my daughter's finger and cut her throat if I did not give him thirty thousand dollars.

He said, "You see, I have your daughter as hostage. Your daughter will be dead if you contact the police or anybody else".

It was somewhat frightening to accept this at the time. Having informed him I had 3.00 dollars in the bank, I listened to him patiently. He hung up after saying, "You better overdraw from your account."

After that, I waited for a bit before leaving the firm since the woman had shut the door out of fear. I answered, "You can open it whatever happens to me; I'm not afraid of my time to pass away." God is in control and will always have the final say.

I appreciate you reading my book "A Wife Fighting Against All Odds". Thanks for being one of my lovely readers.

2018 palm valley

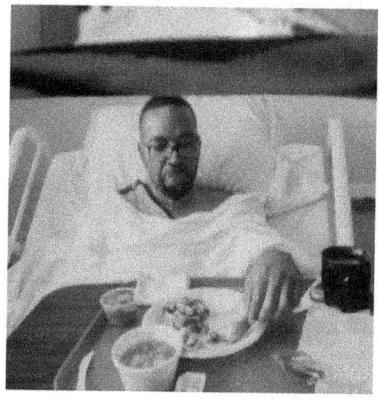

2022 he was in Estrella care center the next day his wife had surgery he was admitted Dec 16 2022, her surgery 12 17

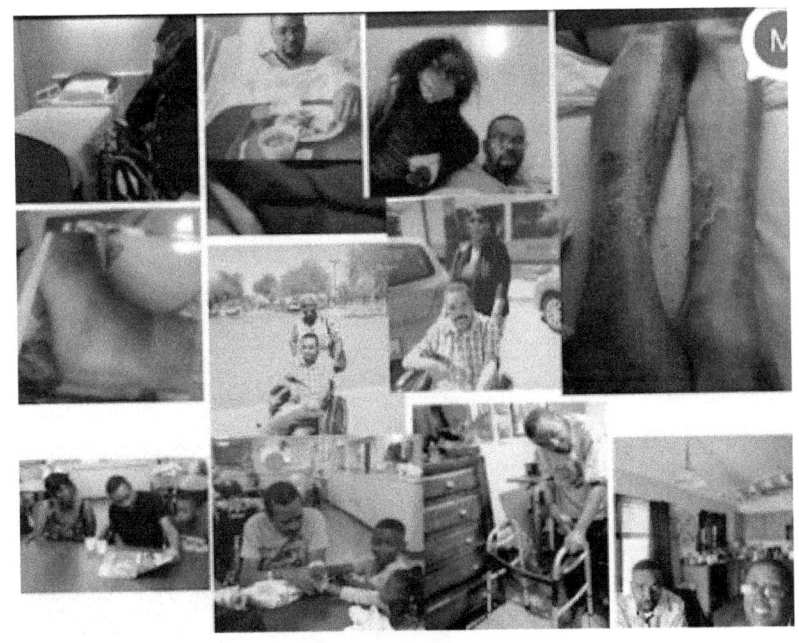

Top of the pages was 2022 and 2023 at

Estrella care

The middle was 2018, standing up 2024 sitting down was recently. Please check on love one, or you can find him like this or worse.

His wife fighting against all the

odds for her husband to make a better outcome for his life. It isn't over until God says it's over.

www.ingramcontent.com/pod-product-compliance
Lightning Source LLC
Chambersburg PA
CBHW051039160426
43193CB00010B/993